I am a Chimpanzee

Aaron Carr

LET'S READ
AV2 BY WEIGL
ADDED VALUE · AUDIO VISUAL

www.av2books.com

AV² provides enriched content that supplements and complements this book. Weigl's AV² books strive to create inspired learning and engage young minds in a total learning experience.

Your AV² Media Enhanced books come alive with...

Audio
Listen to sections of the book read aloud.

Key Words
Study vocabulary, and complete a matching word activity.

Go to www.av2books.com, and enter this book's unique code.

Video
Watch informative video clips.

Quizzes
Test your knowledge.

BOOK CODE

Q306617

Embedded Weblinks
Gain additional information for research.

Slide Show
View images and captions, and prepare a presentation.

AV² by Weigl brings you media enhanced books that support active learning.

Try This!
Complete activities and hands-on experiments.

... and much, much more!

Published by AV² by Weigl
350 5th Avenue, 59th Floor New York, NY 10118
Website: www.av2books.com   www.weigl.com

Library of Congress Cataloging-in-Publication Data
Carr, Aaron.
 Chimpanzee / Aaron Carr.
   pages cm. -- (I am)
 ISBN 978-1-62127-281-6 (hardcover : alkaline paper) -- ISBN 978-1-62127-287-8 (softcover : alkaline paper)
 1. Chimpanzees--Juvenile literature. I. Title.
 QL737.P96C375 2013
 599.885--dc23

                                    2012045443

Printed in the United States of America in North Mankato, Minnesota
1 2 3 4 5 6 7 8 9 0 17 16 15 14 13

032013
WEP300113

Senior Editor: Aaron Carr   Art Director: Terry Paulhus

Weigl acknowledges Getty Images as the primary image supplier for this title.

I am a Chimpanzee

In this book, I will teach you about

- myself
- my food
- my home
- my family

and much more!

I am a chimpanzee.

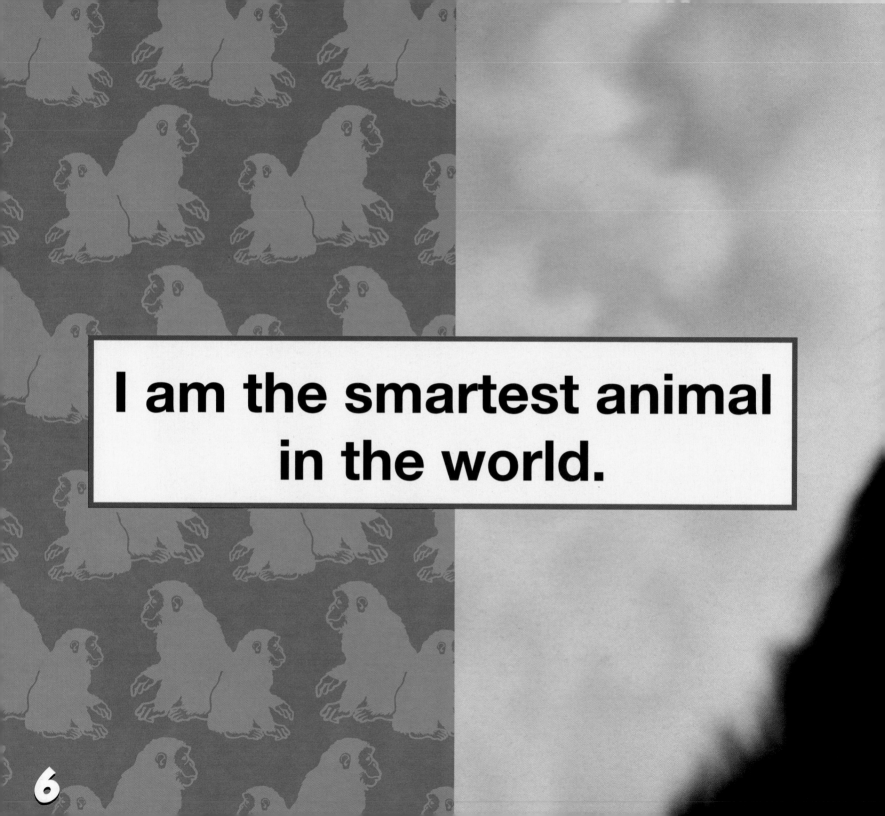

I am the smartest animal in the world.

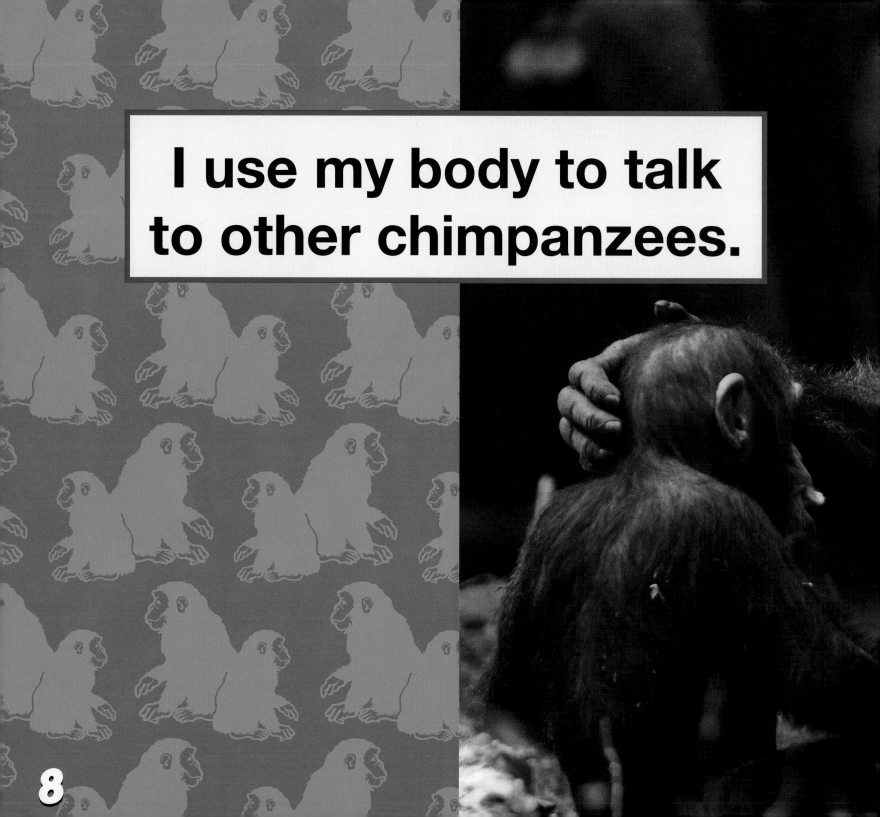

I use my body to talk to other chimpanzees.

8

I eat about 300 different kinds of foods.

I have arms
that are longer
than my legs.

I spend most of my time high up in trees.

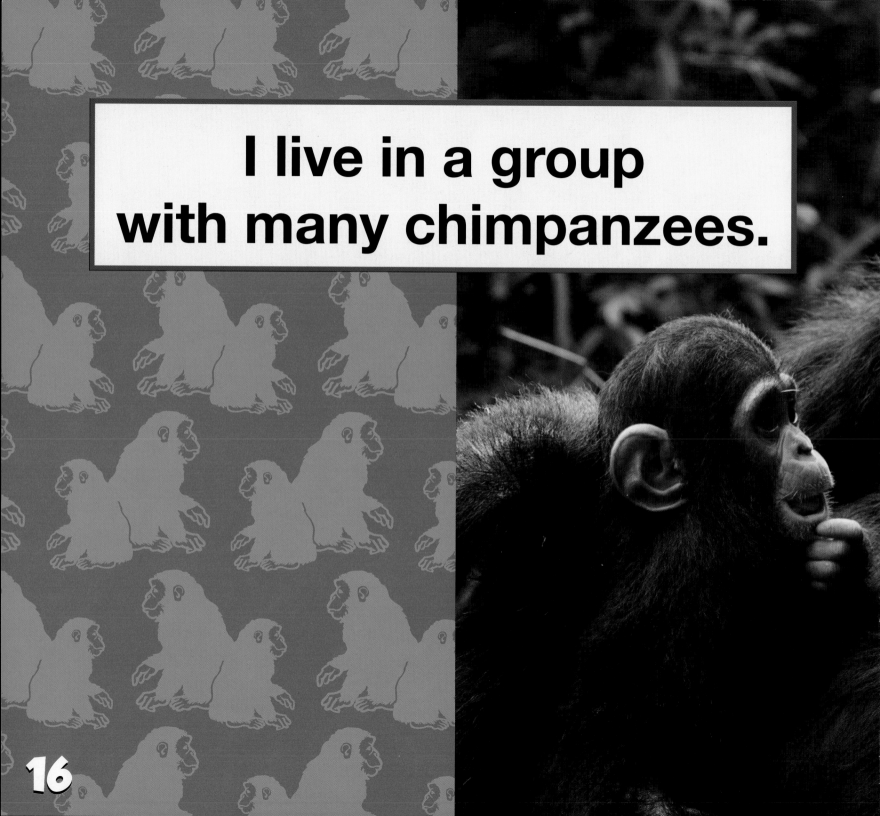

I live in a group
with many chimpanzees.

16

I rode on my mother's back when I was a baby.

I live in the rain forests of Africa.

I am a chimpanzee.

CHIMPANZEE FACTS

These pages provide detailed information that expands on the interesting facts found in the book. They are intended to be used by adults as a learning support to help young readers round out their knowledge of each amazing animal featured in the *I Am* series.

Pages 4–5

I am a chimpanzee. The chimpanzee is the species of ape most closely related to humans. Humans and chimpanzees share 98 percent of their DNA. Chimpanzees are between 4 and 5.5 feet (1.2 to 1.7 meters) tall. Their weight can range from 70 to 130 pounds (32 to 60 kilograms).

Pages 6–7

I am the smartest animal in the world. Aside from humans, scientists believe chimpanzees are the smartest animals in the world. They are able to solve complex puzzles and even learn sign language. Chimpanzees often use tools. They will use sticks to "fish" for insects, and rocks to crack open nuts.

Pages 8–9

I use my body to talk to other chimpanzees. Chimpanzees communicate with body gestures and by making noises, such as hoots, grunts, and roars. Chimpanzees also express emotion with their faces. They smile when happy, pucker their lips when worried, and bare their teeth when scared.

Pages 10–11

I eat about 300 different kinds of foods. Chimpanzees are omnivores. They prefer to eat plants such as fruit, leaves, seeds, and flowers. They also eat insects, such as ants and termites. Sometimes, they will even hunt small animals, such as monkeys, for their meat.

Pages 12–13

I have arms that are longer than my legs. Chimpanzees have long fingers, which they can use like hooks to grasp trees. They also have opposable thumbs on their hands and feet. Chimpanzees often walk using both their feet and hands. This is called knuckle walking.

Pages 14–15

I spend most of my time high up in trees. Chimpanzees may swing from tree to tree for short distances. If they have to travel longer distances, however, they walk on the ground. They sleep in nests, which they construct in trees. They also find most of their food in trees.

Pages 16–17

I live in a group with many chimpanzees. Chimpanzees live in groups called communities. A community contains from 10 to more than 100 members. A community's territory can be hundreds of square miles (square kilometers) in size.

Pages 18–19

I rode on my mother's back when I was a baby. Newborn chimpanzees weigh about four pounds (1.8 kg). They are completely helpless, relying on their mothers for food, shelter, and protection. Chimpanzees are weaned by about five years old. They are fully mature by 13 to 16 years old.

Pages 20–21

I live in the rain forests of Africa. Chimpanzee populations have been greatly reduced through habitat loss and hunting. Much of their natural habitat has been destroyed due to logging and expanding human settlements. Chimpanzees are also hunted for meat, called "bushmeat." More than 5 million tons (4.5 million metric tons) of bushmeat is taken from the Congo Basin forests each year.

KEY WORDS

Research has shown that as much as 65 percent of all written material published in English is made up of 300 words. These 300 words cannot be taught using pictures or learned by sounding them out. They must be recognized by sight. This book contains 35 common sight words to help young readers improve their reading fluency and comprehension. This book also teaches young readers several important content words, such as proper nouns. These words are paired with pictures to aid in learning and improve understanding.

Page	Sight Words First Appearance	Page	Content Words First Appearance
4	a, am, I	4	chimpanzee
6	animal, in, the, world	8	body
8	my, other, talk, to, use	12	arms, legs
10	about, different, eat, foods, kinds, of	18	baby, mother's
12	are, have, than, that	20	Africa, rain forests
14	high, most, time, trees, up		
16	group, live, many, with		
18	back, on, was, when